KU-406-028

Cows

Tessa Potter and Donna Bailey

MACMILLAN

The farmer on this farm
has a lot of cows.
He keeps them for their milk.

2

He milks them twice a day when
their udders are full of milk.

In summer the cows live
in a field.
They eat the grass.

But in the winter they live
in a cowshed.
The farmer must feed them.

The farmer gives the cows
hay to eat.
He gives them fresh water
to drink.

6

The farmer keeps the cowshed
very clean.
He takes away the dirty straw.
He gives the cows clean dry straw
to lie on.

Look at this cow.

She is very fat.

She will soon have a calf.

The calf has just been born.
It lies on the grass
beside its mother.

The cow licks her new calf.
The calf is soon clean and dry.

10

The calf tries to stand up.

Its legs are very wobbly.

It is hungry.

It wants some milk.

The cow's udder is full of milk
for her new calf.
The calf drinks her warm milk.

When a calf is five days old the farmer
takes it away from its mother.
This girl is teaching a young calf
to drink milk from a bucket.

The calf soon learns to drink
from the bucket.
It does not need milk from
its mother now.

The calf grows fast.
Now it is three weeks old.
It can eat the grass in the field.

There is another calf in the field.
The calves play together and
grow big and strong.

The calves do not drink milk now.
The farmer can have the cows' milk.
The cows eat lots of grass and
they make a lot of milk
for the farmer.

It is milking time.

The cows' udders are full of milk.

They wait for the farmer
at the gate.

18

The farmer fetches the cows
from the field.
They walk in a long line
to the milking shed.

The cows wait outside
the milking shed.
They go in one by one.

20

The first cows go into the stalls
in the shed.
The farmer gives them some food.

21

Each cow stands quietly in her stall.
She eats her food.

The farmer washes her udder.
No dirt must get into the milk.

The farmer has a machine
to milk his cows.

The machine sucks the milk out
from their udders.
It takes ten minutes to milk each cow.

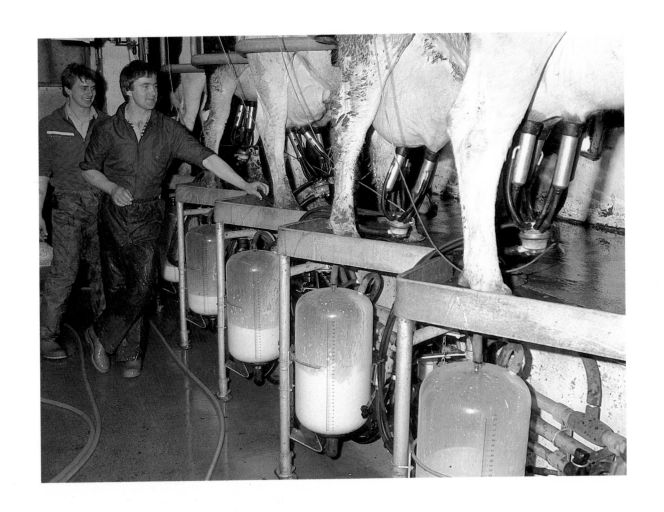

The milk goes into jars.
There are marks on each jar so that
the farmer can see how much milk
each cow has made.

When the cow has no more milk in her udder, the farmer takes away the machine.

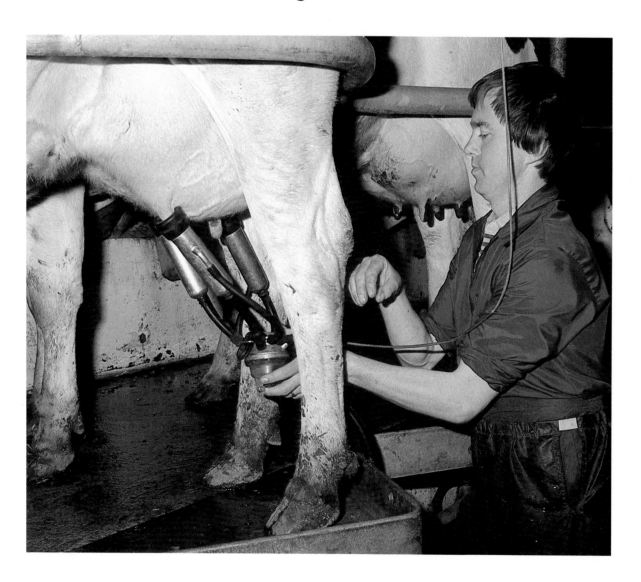

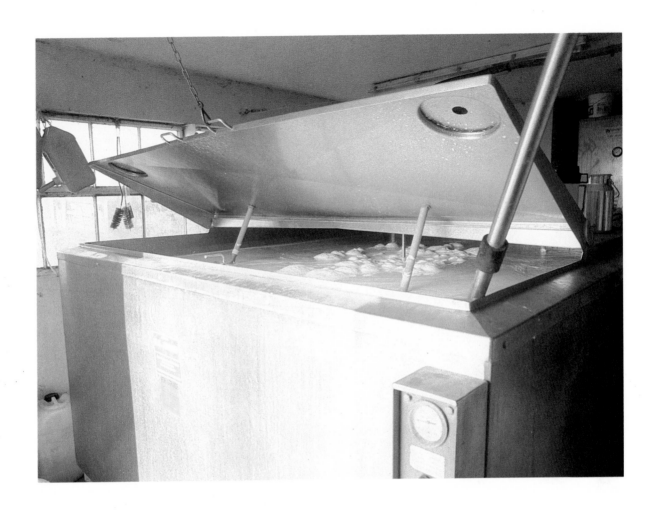

The milk from the jars is pumped
into a big tank.
The milk stays fresh and cold
in the tank.

The cows go back to their field.
Then the farmer washes the milking shed.
He keeps everything very clean.

A milk tanker comes to the farm every day.

It pumps the milk out of the tank.

It takes the milk to the dairy.

30

The milk is put into bottles and cartons in the dairy.
Then caps are put on the bottles and the cartons are closed tight.

A lorry takes the milk from the dairy
to the shops.
Now we can buy the milk to drink.

Reading consultant: Diana Bentley
Editorial consultant: Donna Bailey

Illustrated by Paula Chasty
Picture research by Suzanne Williams
Designed by Richard Garratt Design

This edition specially produced for
Macmillan Children's Books,
a division of Macmillan Publishers Limited

First published 1989

This edition published by
Macmillan Children's Books,
a division of Macmillan Publishers Limited
4 Little Essex Street, London WC2R 3LF and Basingstoke
Associated companies around the world.

Printed in Hong Kong

British Library Cataloguing in Publication Data
Potter, Tessa
    Cows
    1.   Livestock : Dairy Cattle : Cows - For children
    I.   Title II.   Bailey, Donna   III.   Series
    636.2'142
    ISBN 0-333-48660-9

Photographs
Cover: Bruce Coleman/Eric Crichton
Farmers Weekly: 31
Frank Lane Picture Agency: 15 (N Elkins), 16 (Michael Clark)
Peter Greenland: 1, 4, 5, 6, 7, 8, 17, 18, 19, 22, 23, 24, 25, 26, 27,
        28, 29, 30 and 32
Eric and David Hosking: 13 and 14
NHPA: 9, 10, 11 and 12 (Joe B Blossom)